Poems by
Mike Bonikowsky

Solum Literary Press
Norman, OK

© Mike Bonikowsky, 2021

All rights reserved. No part of this publication may be reproduced in any form without the prior written permission of Mike Bonikowsky, except in the case of quotations in critical reviews or other noncommercial uses permitted by copyright law.

Cover art by Sarah Christolini
Cover and interior design by Hannah Thigpen

ISBN: 978-1-7359984-5-9

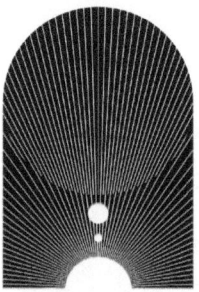

Solum Literary Press
4113 W Main St, Apt J
Norman, OK 73072
info@solumpress.com

For The Small Belonging To God

Contents

Invocation	2
Psalm For Sinking	3
Cormorant Lord	4
Seed-Song	5
Anxieties	6
Maranatha In March	7
Pandemic Hymn	8
RIP Jean Vanier	9
Mother Hen	10
Sharps Disposal	11
Psalm for Lately	12
Martyrs	13
A Secret	14
Doomscrolling	15
Act Of God	16
Red Stuff	17
Trans-Canada	18
Maranatha In September	19
Hollow Psalm	20
The Wilderness Of Other People	21
Ryan In The Woods	22
Canis Familiaris	24
Wildfire Sky	25
Conductor	26
Benediction	27

Acknowledgements

"Cormorant Lord", "Anxieties", "Martyrs", "Ryan In The Woods", "Canis Familiaris", and "Psalm For Sinking" previously appeared in *Love Is Moving Magazine*.

"Pandemic Hymn", "Doomscrolling", and "Trans-Canada" (as "Along Highway 61") previously appeared in *Ekstasis Magazine*.

"Conductor" first appeared in McMaster University Divinity School's *Poems for Ephesians* series.

"Wildfire Sky" first appeared in *Solum Journal Vol. II*.

Red Stuff

Invocation

Sing to the Lord from your unroofed cathedral,
Sing to the Lord from your half-built heart.
Sing to the Lord, all ye mid-restoration,
Sing to the Lord, all ye falling apart.

Psalm For Sinking

Sink, you stones, and be not afraid,
To go the whole way down.
Make your bed beneath the waters,
For He broods over them.

Let yourself be shaped and tumbled
In the depth and darkness.
For though the current's swift and cold,
The shapes it makes are smooth.

The hand may pick you up again,
To fill some hollow place,
In altar, arch, or sling, but
Again, the hand may not.

And if your calling's to be shaped
By time and troubled water,
Then you'll be smooth beneath His feet
When the riverbeds are raised.

Cormorant Lord

I gave my heart to the cormorant Lord,
Who gave me His body for bread.
So how can I be anything less
Than also for the devouring?

So I hold my hungry children close
As they tear the weave of me,
And pierce the cage that holds my heart
To eat whatever is found there.

As I bless their bloody heads,
And ask of my cormorant Lord
That when they eat of me,
They will also eat of Him.

Seed-Song

Lay me down beneath the earth,
And I won't care if I'm buried
Or sown,
So long as Your hands hold the shovel.

Pour the rain down on me,
And I won't care if I'm baptized,
Or drowned,
So long as Your hands hold me under.

Cut me down when harvest comes,
Be it for the burning
Or the barn,
So long as Your hands gather me.

Anxieties

All the lights are coming on:
"Fuel Low," "Service Engine Soon,"
Transmission, tire pressure and
Every other kind of doom.

The light on the thermometer,
"Minimum Payment Due,"
Pushing notifications
That just keep on pushing through.

The forecast's all for heat alerts,
The apps are all for war;
The warnings sound for everything
They make a warning for.

So put thou the car in neutral,
Commit thy smartphone to the deep.
Though the watchmen watch in vain,
He gives to his beloved sleep.

Maranatha In March

Come quickly, Lord.
Kill us with the sight of You.
Raise us by the sound of Your voice.
Call all the old sad earth home,
To weep its weary heart out at Your knee.

Pandemic Hymn

Be not afraid!
Of the numbers on the news,
Rumours in the ransacked aisle,
Horror stories in your head.

If the worst-case comes to pass
And the prophets played it safe,
If the doomsday clock is slow
And the preppers underprepared,

Then we'll all be side by side
Tucked into our lime pit
And resting from our troubles
When He stands upon the earth.

Come again, our lonely Lord,
To sift the nations' ruin,
The ashes of our glory,
For the only thing You'd miss.

If it takes a thousand years,
He'll find our every fragment.
Every tooth for every skull,
Sort out your bones from hers, and mine.

He'll knit us back together,
Every single numbered hair.
He'll call us out of the earth,
Every body by its name.

Be not afraid!
So the angels always say,
Who have seen how humans die,
And what humans are raised to.

RIP Jean Vanier

What death sleeps within my heart?
Let me die before it wakes
To shake to the foundations
Everything I ever made
And make my every word a clanging.

What death sleeps within my heart?
I have a hypothesis
That is enough to bury
All the times that I was nice
And the handful I was good.

What death sleeps within my heart?
Let me die before it wakes,
Write with ashes on my head
And nail my coffin shut, lest
From this Christlike dream I rise.

Mother Hen

Because the nest is soiled,
And the heat lamp is not shared.
Because the grain goes all to those
That don't need any more.

Because the small grow smaller, while
The large grow large enough
To push their weaker brothers
To the foxes and the rats.

She comes again, the mother hen;
Who broods but broods no longer,
Called by the squabble, and the stench, and
The blood beneath the nest she made.

She comes to break the pecking order,
To end their warring with her weight.
The shadow of her wings is wide,
Her peace is soft and heavy.

She comes again, that mother hen,
Who broods, but broods no longer.
She comes to gather, for she knows
What is not gathered is destroyed.

Sharps Disposal

When I was young, I asked to be
A spear in the hand of the Lord;
And if I couldn't be a spear,
I asked that I would be His sword.

I'm older now, and I have seen
Exactly what a spear can do;
What becomes of those who live
By the swords they say are You.

So make of me a warm wet rag,
To wipe the blood and filth away;
And make of me a tourniquet,
To keep the rush of death at bay.

If I must tear my brother's flesh,
If I must make my sister bleed,
Make me a needle in Your hand,
When You the Surgeon intercede.

Psalm for Lately

Praise the Lord!
Praise Him, you anxieties,
Praise Him, you intrusive thoughts,
Praise Him, all ye mental illness.

Praise the Lord, ye burning forests,
Praise Him, all rising oceans,
Praise Him all ye hurricanes,
Let all creation praise Him in its groaning.

Praise Him, all ye variants,
Praise Him, rising interest rates,
Praise Him, unemployment,
Praise Him with loud praise, ye busted muffler.

Praise Him, noonday demon,
Praise Him, terrors in the night
Who only chase us back to Him
Who has put all things beneath His feet

But us upon His shoulders.

Martyrs

When the Facebook bell starts ringing
To tell of more lives taken
By men with names that are not like ours,
You always say the same thing
Time after time after time.

That they are monsters and
Inhuman and cannot
Be comprehended
For they are not like us,
No brother, not at all.

But I say, brother, you're a liar,
And maybe sister, you forgot
The things we used to say in high school,
The songs we sang when we were young,
A little too in love with easeful death.

And I say how fortunate are we
And the heretics we hated
And the infidels we feared
And I say thank Christ He made it clear
Which end of the gun we are to stand on.

A Secret

Down by the county road,
Playing little boy games,
Waiting for the school bus,
My son looks up and says,

"I want to tell you something."
I lean down so he can
whisper it in my ear:
Then, "I hate you, Daddy."

Just to taste the words come out,
Just to watch the knife go in.
Just to watch my face change,
As I feel it.

So don't tell me that we
Can make it if we try,
Because he's just like his daddy
And his daddy's just like his.

Doomscrolling

I read the stories this world tells,
As they go scrolling by,
And every story I am told
Is worse than the one before.

I am told that I must respond:
Speak my piece, give my take.
Plant my flag here, or maybe there,
One side or the other.

But all I see is my beloved,
Crucified by my beloved.
All I can say is to the hills, "Cover us"
And to the mountains, "Fall on us."

Act Of God

Come quickly, Lord,
To kick the doors
Out of my locked
And alarmed heart.

Fill every room:
Beds with weary,
Tables with starved,
Silence with song.

All buildings burn
Down in the end.
Let my ruins
Be a temple.

Red Stuff

Down by the river, my little son
Is snapping twigs and tossing them
To see the runoff carry them.
I watch til my mind wanders off.

"What's that red stuff?" I hear him say.
I look down absently to see
His white star-fingers staining red,
With a thing he has no word for.

He is not afraid to taste it
And the pain has yet to arrive.
I see the moment when it does,
And I watch his face grow older.

When tears dry and the wound is bound
I teach him what the red stuff's called,
Sitting under that old tree,
Swearing we won't eat this time.

Trans-Canada

Bring up the jackhammer of the Lord,
And find a cleft to set the chisel.
For nothing's ever grown here
And the highway's coming through.

But if the bit can't find a purchase
On my metamorphic heart,
Bring up the drills of heaven
And get straight to boring down.

Fill Your holy boreholes
With Your sacred high explosive,
Set to blow the living hell
Out of my rock-hard heart.

Strip my false and alloyed self
Of its so-called precious metal.
Leave me an exhausted quarry,
Hollowed and open to the sky.

Then strike the labour camps.
Let return the northern silence,
Call the lichens back to grow
On the broken fragments of the Shield.

Call Your thunderheads across the lake,
Call Your springs up from beneath.
Fill my wound with cold clean waters,
Waters still and dark and deep.

Come make of my blessed hollow
A place where creatures drink their fill.
A place where children swim and play
When the land is hot and dry.

Maranatha In September

Oh won't You come back
And show us, Your children,
How we're all wrong,
How we're alright.

Oh won't You come back,
Put an end to this recess.
Take the sticks from the bullies,
Wipe the tears from our eyes.

Oh won't You come back,
And teach us to share:
Rightly dividing the cookies and juice,
The hats, the mittens, and the boots.

Oh won't You come back
And make us say sorry.
End the calling of all names,
Save the one upon the stone.

Oh won't You come back
And say the day's over.
Let the bell ring that says
That it's time to go home.

Hollow Psalm

I go down to the county road,
There to meet the yellow bus:
Son in right hand, daughter left
Masked in primary colours.

The bus comes to bear them to
Their semi-sanitized school,
And I am left there alone
With today's apocalypse.

Sky should be blue, but isn't;
Sun should be gold, but instead
A dull red eye is glaring
Through smoke from California.

Not a word left in my mouth,
Nor meditation in my heart.
Empty as I've ever been,
Hollowed out, and then scraped clean.

Send me a lamentation
From behind the wildfire sun,
Oil from my emptiness.
Psalm to sing, with covered mouth.

You made me to be hollow,
Now make me to be filled
If only to be poured out,
Once more before the breaking.

The Wilderness Of Other People

Christ have mercy, for we go
Into the wilderness of other people
To bear the blazing of their gaze
And the night of their indifference.

Christ have mercy, as we bear
The hard rain of other hearts:
The autumn sun of knowing,
The winter wind of being known.

Christ have mercy, for we fear
The wilderness of other people.
And we come, with axe and flame,
To make a place we recognize.

Christ have mercy, we've become
A wilderness of other people.
Lost in ourselves, on our way to a place
Where the other is not other anymore.

Ryan In The Woods

Ryan loved water
That Christmas when I worked with him.
He would take my hand and pull me
Out the institution door
Down through the forest
To where the river ran.

It was Toronto in December
And the dirty woods were grim
But there was nothing else he wanted
From his long blank day,
And Ryan was blind
And needed hands to guide him there.

He was laughing as I led him
Down the narrow path
Through the ruined city woods
By the highway,
The haunt of prostitutes
Down by the addict's Humber.

He held my hand and followed me
Down to the river,
Roaring brown with winter rain
And he stood there
And forgot me
And listened to it roar, at last.

When it grew cold we turned to go
Back up through the forest
To the institution,
Brick red upon the hill
To lunch, and a bath, and Barney,
Though I could not tell him so.

So we were halfway home
When Ryan turned on me,
Inner tides reversing,
Inner weather growing grim;
His laughter ceasing, and
Turning over into rage.

His face a wordless curse,
He began to scratch
With ragged nails
To strike with foot and fist
At the one who led him,
Through what he couldn't see.

So I pull Ryan through the woods
Threading the narrow path
As he spits and strikes at me.
He is being led
To the doors of warmth and safety
That he cannot see.

And I can't be angry,
And I can't be surprised,
For daily I am blind
And daily I rage
And daily I wound
The hand that leads me.

Canis Familiaris

Come on, wolf, and let us play,
Though all my days you've stalked me,
Through every hour of my life,
Down every hall and highway.

Come, let us race and chase and
Roll and tumble intertwined.
I cannot escape you, and
You cannot devour me.

Come on, wolf, and chase me home
To where the lion and the lamb,
Mental illness and the man
Lie down in peace together.

Wildfire Sky

Come let us walk together,
Beneath the wildfire sky,
Into the unread pages
At the end of the story.

There is no weapon
That can defend against what comes,
So let's drop our therapeutic arms
And live with open hands.

There are no tools of ours
That can mend what has been broken,
So let's drop our anxious hammers
And receive what is given.

There are no words of ours
That can spell what is away,
So let us shut our mouths
And listen.

Oh God, oh God, lift up our eyes.
Oh God shut up our mouths,
Take us by our empty hands,
And lead us where we would not go.

Conductor

When it comes down, it comes down
Out of the dark heart of the nimbus.
I can never see it coming
Until I can see nothing else.

It finds my outstretched fingers,
Travels down my reaching arms
To turn my bones to filaments,
And makes my heart to burn.

I should be obliterated,
Made so mortal a conductor
Of so furious a light,
But He grounded me before He struck

And being struck, I glow.

Benediction

Blessed be the name of the Lord!

Lord over the laughing child,
And over school's last day.
Lord over their long delight,
And their unending play.

Lord of the dripping morphine,
And the necrotic sore.
Lord of the catheter bag,
And the unopened door.

Lord of the daughters of Lot,
And sons of Abraham.
Lord of His forsaken Self,
For whom He sends no ram.

Lord of the unanswered cry,
And of the lonely bed.
Lord Who came to be with us,
Both the living and the dead.

Blessed be the name of the Lord.

About the Author

Mike Bonikowsky lives in Melancthon, Ontario with his wife and kids. He works as a caregiver for men and women with developmental disabilities and writes poems when necessary.

www.ingramcontent.com/pod-product-compliance
Lightning Source LLC
Chambersburg PA
CBHW020133130526
44590CB00040B/615